THINKING
outside
the BLOCK

Step by Step to Dynamic Quilts

Sandi Cummings with Karen Flamme

To Karen —
Have a great time
quilting!
Sandi Cummings

C&T PUBLISHING

Text and artwork © 2004 Sandi Cummings with Karen Flamme
Artwork ©2004 C&T Publishing

Publisher: Amy Marson
Editorial Director: Gailen Runge
Editor: Cyndy Lyle Rymer
Technical Editor: Gailen Runge
Copyeditor/Proofreader: Diane Kennedy-Jackson/Eva Simoni Erb
Cover and Book Design: Kristy A. Konitzer
Illustrator: Gailen Runge
Production Assistant: Matt Allen
Quilt Photography: Sharon Risedorph unless otherwise noted
How-to Photography: Diane Pedersen unless otherwise noted
Published by C&T Publishing, Inc., P.O. Box 1456, Lafayette, California, 94549

Front cover: *Sunrise,* Sandi Cummings. Photo by Sharon Risedorph
Back cover: *Untitled* and *Playtime,* Sandi Cummings

Library of Congress Cataloging-in-Publication Data

Cummings, Sandi.
  Thinking outside the block : step by step to dynamic quilts / Sandi Cummings with Karen Flamme.
       p. cm.
Includes bibliographical references and index.
  ISBN 1-57120-238-2 (paper trade)
  1. Quilts—Design. 2. Art quilts. I. Flamme, Karen. II. Title.

TT835.C855 2004
746.46'041—dc21

                                        2003011824

Printed in China
10 9 8 7 6 5 4 3 2

Acknowledgments

This is the only section of the book where the writing has been left entirely to me. And thank heavens! I would rather spend my time in the studio in front of my sewing machine than at the computer. For this reason I am very grateful to Karen. We spent many long hours together talking and working so she might skillfully represent my thoughts and techniques. I appreciate her sense of organization, reliability, and thoroughness.

There are always friends and family behind the scenes, and I am fortunate to have support from both. My number one advocate is my husband, Gary. He has always understood my need to create and has continually encouraged me.

I smile as I think of my daughter and son, Tracy and Ryan, who have unwittingly accepted quilting as an implied part of their lives. Besides their support, they bring me fabric treasures from their treks around the world.

I am also grateful to my son-in-law, Chip, who has helped bring me into the twenty-first century by sharing his computer knowledge. I have always relied on the friendship of Thorley Murray and Susan Turner. They supply me with unending enthusiasm, kind words, and a critical eye. I am one lucky person!

Sandi Cummings

Writing this book has been a delight. Creating art quilts and writing about them combines my life-long fascination with color, design, texture, fiber arts, and communication. On one level Sandi's work speaks for itself and needs no words in order to be enjoyed and appreciated. On another level there is much to be learned from the exploration into color and design and the freedom of experimentation she teaches us.

As a child I slept under quilts made by my grandmother and loved to hear my mother's stories about whose shirts and dresses supplied the fabric. But making quilts was another matter. The precision and repetition of traditional quilting were a challenge both for my dexterity and my temperament. A class given by Sandi at a local fabric store started me on the art quilt journey. Sandi was a long-time friend whose work I had admired for years, and she assured me her class would be fun and not intimidating. She was right, but she didn't warn me that it was also addicting. As you read these pages and complete the projects you will find your creative spark igniting as I did mine. And I'm sure you will also find joy in knowing you have made something that is uniquely yours.

Sandi has made writing this book an easy, fun task. I have learned and laughed far more than I have labored over it. Sandi is generous with her encouragement, time, and knowledge. Her spirit and enthusiasm for artistic experimentation are contagious.

My family has been incredibly generous also. My husband John patiently trades visits to fabric stores for stops at hardware stores (I think I owe him a few!). And I rely on my daughter Jennifer and her unfailing eye for excellence to find the trouble spot in a quilt or the sentence that needs fixing. They both believe in me long before I do and encourage my whims without hesitation.

Karen Flamme

3

table of contents

Preface

I began quilting during the late 1970s somewhat by accident. My intention was to take a stained-glass class at the local community center, but the class was full. Instead, I signed up for a quilting class and thus began my introduction to traditional quilting. I liked selecting the fabrics and watching something new emerge by stitching the colors and patterns of cloth together. I realized there was something very seductive about working with fabric. Soon I was bundling my two small children, Tracy and Ryan, into the car for trips to San Francisco in search of the new "pin-dot" or calico I heard was available there. I spent late nights tracing templates of triangles or squares, hoping I would have time to piece them all. Needless to say, that stained-glass window never got made and my fascination with quilting grew unbounded. Soon I needed more space in the house and more space in my life for this passion.

During the 1970s, most quiltmakers had a singular vision: to re-create many of the quilts of the past. But the quilting world was changing, and quilts acquired a new dimension. They were no longer artistic expressions that had to be functional and relegated to the bed. They were beginning to be seen as art that could be displayed on the wall. This was a major shift in attitude, and with that shift, quiltmakers began to feel freer to express themselves in a less traditional manner. It wasn't long before my creative outlook, and my quilts, began to change. I followed my urge to start deviating from the norm and to move away from precision piecing and templates.

The evolution of the art quilt has been made easier by the new materials and techniques available. We color our own fabrics with a wide variety of paints, dyes, discharge pastes, stenciling, and screen-printing materials. We have the option of using quart jars, plastic bags, and trays to dye our fabrics rather than lugging around five gallon buckets filled with water. Technology offers new techniques we can use to transfer photos and other images to fabric. And who can remember life before the rotary cutter?

Much of the work we are doing today in contemporary quilting would not have been possible without these advances. For many of us, our work evolved as we experimented with the new materials as soon as they were available.

Today, the myriad possibilities and techniques available can be overwhelming to a quilter who is attempting to cross the line from traditional to contemporary quilting. It's similar to walking into a market filled with foreign foods; they all look interesting and you know they have the potential to make something delicious, but where do you start and how do you use them?

This book offers projects and guidance for getting started in unfamiliar territory. It shows you some techniques and methods of working that I have found helpful. I hope it encourages you to play, and inspires you to keep trying new ideas. You won't find a lot of rules in this book because the second I make a rule, someone does it the opposite way and makes something wonderful. That's why it's important to go with your own impulses. Have confidence that as you work you will be bombarded with all sorts of ideas of your own.

The key to success with this book is to experiment. Try things and don't worry about how successful you are when you first begin. In my garage I have boxes of failed experiments, but they are all valuable because they taught me many lessons. Every quilt builds on those that came before it, and with each quilt your confidence and perception will grow. You will master the techniques and eventually discover your own style and vision.

thinking
outside the block

Blocks are familiar, symmetrical shapes that are all around us. Babies play with them, skyscrapers are made of them, and quilters dissect, manipulate, twist, turn, name, and rename them.

When I started quilting over twenty years ago, I made traditional quilts using familiar blocks and patterns. I entered one of these early quilts in a quilt show. During a visit to the show I experienced what I refer to as an "Ah-ha" moment; a definite turning point in my quilting career. As I entered the hall I walked right past my own soft-colored traditional quilt, I was drawn to a nearby quilt with strong, dynamic colors and a unique layout. Suddenly I found my own quilt uninteresting and ordinary. The other quilt had captured my interest because it was vibrant, lively, and full of motion. I knew right then that I wanted to be making quilts that expressed my individuality and were full of energy.

Of course there's a big difference between wanting to do something and knowing how to do it. So I started with something familiar, the block, and began experimenting. I made traditional blocks but used unusual fabrics. For one quilt I made star blocks in different sizes and played with them to add spark and individuality. I cut off some corners, inserted strips, and brainstormed other ideas.

I worked within the block format because it was comfortable and familiar, but stretched tradition to make the squares more unusual and more interesting to me. Needless to say, I have continued to experiment, and no two of my quilts are ever alike. I may "waste" time and fabric as I continue to learn, but this process of discovery is still fascinating to me. I approach my quiltmaking as a continual process of color exploration and design experimentation.

I've learned from teaching other quilters that getting started is often the most challenging step in trying to cross the bridge from traditional to more contemporary quilts. Students tell me that once they make it over that initial hurdle the experience is freeing, and they find the variations are limitless and full of surprises.

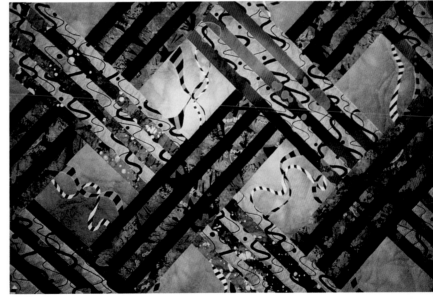

This design is based on a 6" square.

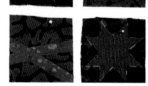

My goal is to help you get started by encouraging you to try new things with familiar shapes. The projects rely on the basic design strength of the block unit as a springboard for making contemporary quilts. Most of these quilts are made as wallhangings. They don't follow a prescribed pattern. You are given plenty of leeway to add your own creativity and individuality. You will learn to design as you go and to experiment. I think you will be surprised and delighted by the results of your efforts.

Here are some basic points I continually emphasize throughout the book. I believe they are the keys to success.

Trust in your own creativity; it's there waiting to be tapped.

It's okay and even necessary to waste time and fabric because you're learning as you go.

Be flexible and open to surprises; this is how discoveries happen.

There are no patterns to follow, no templates to cut, and, best of all, there are no rules.

Have fun and don't stress; there is no wrong way to work.

While the idea of venturing out on your own may sound unnerving at first, with a little practice you'll learn to trust your creative instincts.

As you get swept up into the creative process you'll be amazed at how much fun you can have, and your confidence level will increase. The most important thing is you will find that this type of quilting is a satisfying and freeing art form that allows you to express your individuality. I guarantee that you'll never see other quilts exactly like the ones you create.

Repetition

Repetition is all around us in nature and our everyday lives. We can see it in our surroundings, in poetry and prose, music, and in the simple routines of our lives. Repetition has always been a very important aspect of quilting, and I am drawn to it. I think repetition can be calming, yet it can also give a sense of energy, movement, and power. It gives things order and unity. It is a key tool for the quilter. I like to think of quilting as a theme with its many variations. The forms can be altered in some way by color, pattern, size, and texture. In this way the visual impact grows and the quilt becomes more than the sum of its parts.

Photos by Sandi Cummings

make room for creativity

When I titled this chapter, I was thinking of the importance of making room for creativity in both your mind and your workspace. Throughout this book you'll be stretching your imagination as well as changing your usual way of working.

This is a fun, loose style of quilting. There are no rules and there are no wrong ways to work. For most of the projects you don't need to worry about precise measurements and careful cutting. You need to be willing to spend some time and "waste" some fabric as you experiment and try new techniques. The key to success with these projects is to remain flexible and open to surprises, and, most importantly, to approach them with an open mind and trust in your own creativity.

It's easy for us to repeat familiar patterns, colors, and designs in our quilts. Moving out of that safe zone and into a mode of experimentation is harder.

How often do you hear others, or yourself, say "I'm not an artist" or "I'm not creative?" It's easy to feel intimidated by the "artist" label. Maybe you think it implies mastery, and that all of a sudden all your work has to be good. You will find yourself becoming both an artist and a creator as you experiment, explore, and put your own personality into your quilts. You're going to design quilts in these projects, not follow set patterns. As you experiment with fabric choices, placement, transition blocks, and new ways of working, you are training and developing your artistic strengths.

In the past, many people believed that creative ability was something only a few people were born with. Current thinking is that there is creative potential in everyone; creative ability can be developed and enhanced. In *The Artist's Way* Julia Cameron shares a number of wonderful quotes that encourage artistic confidence and productivity. In my workshops I usually read several of these quotes before we begin. I like to reinforce the idea that we are all students of art and all have creative potential; we are just at different stages of our development. This thought helps make the class a safe place to experiment. It gives permission to fail. I think it's a good attitude to keep in mind whenever we are trying to be creative. To put it simply, I think that the key is to just work and keep producing.

The need to be a great artist makes it hard to be an artist. The need to produce a great work of art makes it hard to produce any art at all.

Julia Cameron

For your art to grow you have to be willing to devote regular blocks of time and effort. When I was first quilting, I worked part-time while raising my family; it was difficult to say, for example, that Monday and Wednesday from 9 to 12 I would be creative. I was frustrated, but I learned to set aside time when I could quilt without great expectations. If something new and different came out of it that was great. If not, I was able to relax and enjoy the process and results of just making something fun.

Remember that even if you have made a truly rotten piece of art, it may be a necessary stepping-stone to your next work. Art matures spasmodically and requires ugly-duckling growth stages.
Julia Cameron

Trust that still, small voice that says, 'This might work and I'll try it. Diane Mariechild

One does not discover new lands without consenting to lose sight of the shore for a very long time. André Gide

When I start work on a new quilt I have a basic idea in mind, but I don't have a clear vision of the finished piece. I begin with an idea, some basic blocks or units, and then develop or change them. It's impossible for me to design a whole piece before I begin working on it. If I try to plan too much I become paralyzed. Experience has taught me that I have to trust that the piece will grow and develop, and that ideas will come to me as I work. It's best for me if I just jump in, get started, and let the quilt evolve.

David Bayles and Ted Orland tell a story in *Art & Fear* that deserves repeating:

The ceramics teacher announced on opening day that he was dividing the class into two groups. All those on the left side of the studio, he said, would be graded solely on the quantity of work they produced, all those on the right solely on its quality. His procedure was simple: on the final day of class he would bring in his bathroom scales and weigh the work of the "quantity" group: 50 lbs. of pots rated an "A," 40 lbs. a "B," and so on. Those being graded on "quality," however, needed to produce only one pot—albeit a perfect one—to get an "A." Well, came grading time and a curious fact emerged: the works of highest quality were all produced by the group being graded for quantity. It seems that while the "quantity" group was busily churning out piles of work—and learning from their mistakes—the "quality" group had sat theorizing about perfection, and in the end had little more to show for their efforts than grandiose theories and a pile of dead clay....To require perfection is to invite paralysis.

Claiming Your Space

Where you work is important because you need to be comfortable and willing to spend time there. I think it's essential that every artist has a specific workspace. Let's call it a studio. Of course the definition of studio may vary widely. It may be part of a spare bedroom, a table you can call your own with a cart to hold your tools, or a well-equipped separate room. The important thing is that it is a space where you can leave your sewing machine, projects, work board, and tools. It should be well lit and uncluttered. Consider surrounding yourself with pictures, colors, and books you find inspiring. In any case, make it a place where you want to go and spend some time.

When we added on to our home to enlarge my working space, I made a conscious decision to call that room my studio. For me it is a mind set or attitude. It implies direction and commitment to goals whether they are personal or professional.

Photo by Diane Pedersen

Quilt rack I designed to fit in a bedroom closet with leftover hanging space for guests to use.

One of the most important features of your studio is an area you can use as a design wall. It can be a lightweight board you move around or something fixed to a wall. A design wall works well if it is covered in flannel, fleece, or, preferably, a gridded design-wall fabric. Working on a design wall may be new to you, but most of the projects in this book are wallhangings meant to be composed on a wall and viewed from a distance as you work.

Even if you're on the right track, you'll get run over if you just sit there.
Will Rogers

Experience taught me the importance of working on a wall. Originally I thought that, if the fabrics in my quilts matched and were harmonious, the quilts would automatically look good. It just doesn't work that way. I was often disappointed when the quilt was completed. It isn't enough that the colors match. Within a palette of complementary colors it's important to have changes in value: lights, mediums, and darks. By working on a design wall I can step back far enough to evaluate contrast, light levels, and variety in scale. The importance of these elements is not always apparent when you are looking at a quilt up close, but it becomes essential when viewing the piece from a distance.

My fabric closet

Fabric Has It All

Is there a quilter who doesn't love to go to a fabric store? Looking at the array of fabrics available makes your mind race with new ideas. Quilters have an enormous range of fabrics to choose from: commercial, hand-dyed, and printed. Fabric has it all: color, pattern, and visual texture. It's also tactile; just the feel and texture of most fabrics is satisfying. Often when I return from a shopping trip I put the new fabrics up on my work wall just to study them and imagine how they might look in a quilt.

When it's time to store the new fabrics on a shelf, I consciously decide where to put them so they will be easy to find. My fabrics are sorted according to style and energy (or emotional) level. Some general categories I include are hand-dyeds, batiks, primary colors, whimsical, traditional, florals, and plaids.

I separate out colors I use consistently, such as yellows or black and whites. When I am working on a quilt this method of organization helps me spot something I may not have specifically looked for, and leads to consideration of a wider spectrum because everything isn't arranged strictly by color. This system encourages me to venture from my comfort zone of accepted color combinations and to try out other fabrics that might work.

Always work with fabrics you love. If you do, even when you are experimenting, your commitment level will be higher. You have a better chance of creating something that you will continue working on and finish. You will also work harder to solve problems that arise. Quilting requires a big investment of time; why compromise on the fabrics you use?

Color is an exciting element of design. It can be subtle and calming or loud and powerful. For an artist it helps express emotion; for the viewer it evokes an emotional response.

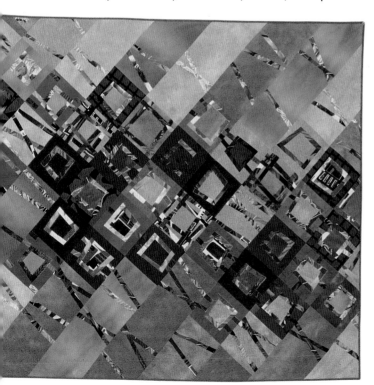

Box Kites, Sandi Cummings, 46" x 40", quilted by Sandy Klop, corporate collection.

Warm or Cool?

Traditionally, reds, oranges, and yellows are referred to as warm colors; blues, greens, and violets or purples are cool colors. Colors can appear to be warmer or cooler depending on the colors near them.

Cool colors with a warm accent

Warm colors with a cool accent

When I place a lot of warm colors on my design wall I have an urge to add something that is cool. I like the contrast it adds and the resulting interest or "spark." My quilts tend to be predominantly warm or cool, and I use the opposite "temperature" as an accent to enhance or enrich the piece. To use both in equal amounts may be disconcerting to the viewer.

No Need to Over Match

I tend to use more colors in my quilts rather than less, and resist the urge to make colors "match" too much. I spend a lot of time selecting the fabrics before beginning a quilt. I usually start with ten or fifteen possibilities; I may not use them all, and I often add others as I work. After choosing fabrics that work well together, I look for something to push things a little—a fabric that still works well with the mix, but is on the edge. I always try to put in a couple of odd-ball fabrics. Avoid being satisfied with your first choices. See if you can add a fabric that works but that will surprise the viewer.

Untitled, Sandi Cummings, 28" x 28", quilted by Sandy Klop, corporate collection. The color combinations in this quilt are unusual but effective. Photo by Sandi Cummings

I hand dye fabrics in large trays to get a smooth transition from one color to another and a good variety in value. The trays are about 30" square, and are intended for use under large appliances such as refrigerators. I use Procion MX dye on fabric that is prepared by the manufacturer for dyeing (see Resources, page 94). The fabric is mercerized combed cotton broadcloth with a high thread count.

The Process

Begin by laying fabric out flat in a tray (fabric can be doubled). Wet fabric and press out all the air bubbles. Pour off excess water.

Prepare dye from dye concentrate and expect to use about ½ to ¾ cup each of two different colors of dye concentrate mixed with water for one yard of fabric. One of my favorite combinations is plum and gold.

Pour both dye colors onto the fabric quickly in several different spots. Wear rubber gloves to move the dye around gently with your hands to blend some areas of the colors.

 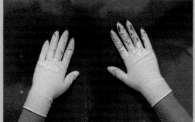
Pour both colors and move dye around.

Finish the process by adding a soda ash solution about 20 minutes later. If possible, let the trays sit out overnight with the fabric in the soda ash solution. Then wash fabric thoroughly in water using Synthrapol (see Resources, page 94).

Low Water Immersion Dyeing Guidelines

These are dye formulas that I learned years ago from Ann Johnston and adapted to dyeing in trays.

To make UREA WATER: Mix 5 tablespoons of urea with 1 measuring cup of warm water. This may be stored at room temperature.

To make SODA ASH WATER: Mix 1 heaping cup of soda ash with 1 gallon water. This may be stored at room temperature.

To make DYE CONCENTRATES: Mix 2 heaping tablespoons of powdered dye with 1 cup of urea water. Do not dissolve dyes in water hotter than 95° F. Dye concentrate must be stored in the refrigerator, and will keep for a few weeks.

APPLICATION OF DYE: Mix to color and value desired, approximately 1 cup of liquid for each yard of fabric.

- **For darker value,** use 4 to 5 teaspoons concentrate and about ¾ cup water.

- **For medium value,** use 2 to 3 teaspoons concentrate and about ¾ cup water.

- **For lighter value,** use only ¼ teaspoon to l teaspoon concentrate and about ¾ cup water.

Walking into a classroom, I frequently notice that students are wearing clothes in the same color range as the fabrics they are working with. Color is a very personal thing. People are attracted to certain colors and certain color combinations. I am addicted to yellow. I love its warmth and light, and all its variations: clear yellows, golden yellows, lemon yellows, orange yellows, and tints and shades. I add a piece of yellow in almost every quilt I am working on. When I consciously try not to use it, I miss it like an old friend. For the time being I have given in to my addiction to yellow. I've gone through many phases in my quilting, and I know I will eventually move on and broaden my color horizon in the future.

The Value of Value

It's difficult to discuss color without talking about value. I believe the viewer responds to value—lights, mediums, and darks—before responding to color. It took a long time to accept that idea because I believed that color was everything. But I realized that if I'm having a problem with a quilt it is usually related to value. I've learned to stand back and study the balance of lights, mediums, and darks. Although it varies with each quilt, typically the medium values that help to unite a piece are missing. If a quilt seems dull, uninteresting, or unbalanced, it usually can be traced to a problem of value differences rather than color.

The response to color is emotional, but value also plays an important role in that response. If you want drama you need the lightest lights and the darkest darks. Sharp contrast in value provides a striking effect. If your goal is a soft, moody quilt, strive for less contrast. You'll still use a combination of lights, mediums, and darks, but within a closer range. Colors are dynamic and play off each other. For example, a fabric you may not have been sure was a "light" appears even lighter when placed next to a darker-valued color.

Usually quilters tend to collect fabrics of a certain value. For example, I'm generally drawn to mediums and darks. Knowing that, I try to buy lights whenever I see some that I like.

I started this quilt as a low contrast, soft piece. As it neared completion it seemed to lack the energy I like, so I added the checkerboards.

Importance of Variety in Scale

Variety in scale is also an important consideration in fabric selection. You can achieve variety either by the scale of prints in the fabric or the size of the units (or blocks) you make. It is important for a quilt to have impact from a distance. It is the variety in scale that draws the viewer in to see the details.

The difference in scale makes these exciting fabric combinations.

How do you select fabrics that go together and that also offer variations in both value and scale? Students often bring a big box of fabric to class to start a quilt. Right away they have trouble knowing which ones to pull out and use. It's very difficult to look at a large pile of fabrics and be able to tell which ones will work together and which won't. I think it's best to begin with two fabrics you really like. Then add other pieces one at a time. With each piece, stand back and ask yourself if the combination is still working. As soon as you add a fabric that is questionable, stop and analyze why it doesn't work. Then you have to make a decision. You can take it out, remove a fabric that conflicts with it, or see if there is something else you can add to bridge the errant fabric.

Creating a Mood

Think about the mood you want your quilt to evoke. Do you want it to be vibrant, whimsical, high energy, sophisticated, restful, or busy? Keep that mood in mind as you select fabrics. In fact, when you choose your first two or three fabrics you start to set the mood. One piece might match in terms of color, but it might change the mood you are trying to achieve. Sometimes a fabric works, but it doesn't really add anything. Try to make each piece count.

When you have assembled fabrics you think work well together, fold the pieces into approximately equal sizes so none dominate except, perhaps, the background fabric. Place them on the floor and view them from a distance. Analyze your selection: Does it have enough value difference, variation in scale, and variety? Is it exciting? Are you pushing the color limits? Are there any odd-balls? Keep working at it, and allow yourself time to make decisions. Fabric selection is the hardest, but most important, part of quiltmaking.

Pin the fabrics to your design wall. Stand back and study them. Does the combination still hold your interest? Are there enough lights, mediums, and darks? Are there fabrics that will add surprises to your finished piece rather than making it predictable?

If you can answer yes, then you're on the way to success. Remember that this is only the beginning. As you work you will most likely add fabrics and eliminate a few. This initial fabric selection gives you a good place to start. Now it's time to move forward and gather the rest of your tools.

Photos by Luke Mulks

These groupings set a definite mood.

Notice how the addition of a fabric can change the mood.

start with
something familiar

Altered Stars, Sandi Cummings, 48" x 48", quilted by Angie Woolman at New Pieces, Albany, CA.

Let's get started on the first project. You can work with many of the tools you already have and just adapt the sizes of the blocks in the projects.

Get Your Supplies Together

You'll need:

A blank design wall, covered in flannel, fleece, or, preferably something with a grid printed on it

Basic quilting supplies: rotary cutter, mat, straightedge and square rulers, pins

Sewing machine in good working condition and iron with steam

Plastic bags to hold the scraps from each project. Don't throw anything away! As you will discover in Chapter 9, leftovers can be put to good use.

The first project is based on a familiar block, the basic Sawtooth Star. You'll make the star blocks in this chapter, then make transition blocks and explore different ways to put them together in the next chapter.

Basic 6" Star Block

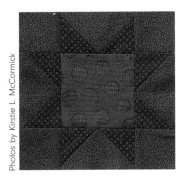

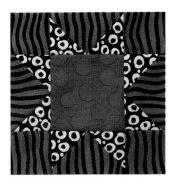

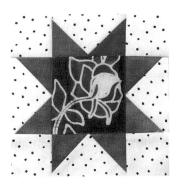
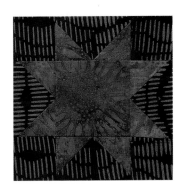

Note: The number of blocks needed for your finished quilt depends on the size quilt you want to make and your choice of layout. The finished quilt is a combination of these star blocks and transition blocks from the following chapter.

Fabric Requirements

Background: approximately 1½-2 yards total

Star points and center square: approximately 1½ yards total

Note: After you make most of your star blocks you will need fabric for the transition blocks, in the next chapter. Wait to choose the fabrics for the transition blocks until you complete most or all of the star blocks. Who knows what you will decide to use in them? As you work you will think of different options. Waiting allows you more latitude with your stars.

Cutting

Instructions are for one star block.

Star center: Cut 1 square 3½" x 3½".

Star points: Cut 1 strip 2" x 16". From this strip cut 8 squares 2" x 2".

Background: Cut 4 rectangles 2" x 3½" and 4 squares 2" x 2".

Making the Block

1. Sew the 2" star-point squares to the 2" x 3½" background rectangles as shown. Trim to a ¼" seam allowance and press.

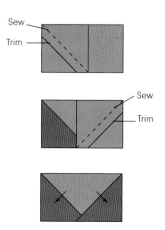

2. Sew the block together as shown. Press as indicated by the arrows. The block should measure 6½" x 6½" square.

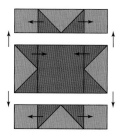

easy
transitions

Now that you have some star blocks ready, you might think your quilt is nearly finished. The idea is to add blocks that infuse the quilt with your individuality. I like to call these transition blocks because they link one star block to another. These blocks also help your quilt make the transition from traditional to contemporary.

Transition blocks add space between the featured blocks. By setting similar blocks right next to each other throughout the quilt, you can lose the beauty of each individual block. I use transition blocks to add depth, motion, and space to my quilts.

Let's start with inserted strips, which make a very simple but effective transition block. The following directions show you how to make one square with inserted strips. As you lay out your star blocks you'll decide where to add transition blocks.

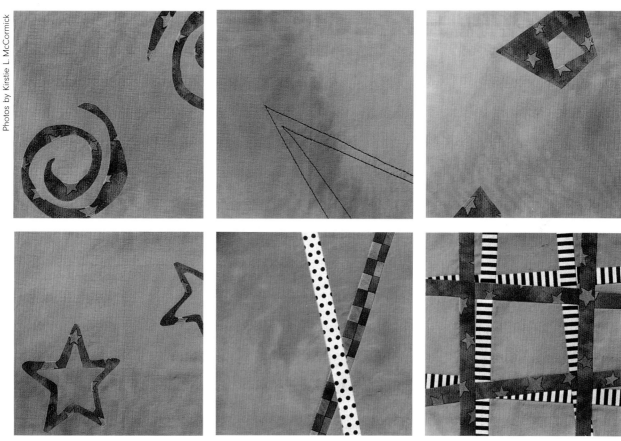

Some ideas for transition blocks

Detail of star quilt with inserted strip blocks

Inserted Strip Block

The instructions are for one block with inserted strips. The number of blocks needed for your quilt depends on the size quilt you want to make and the layout you choose.

Fabric Requirements

A little extra fabric makes life easier. I square the blocks (trimming to 6½" x 6½") after inserting the strips.

Background: 1½–2 yards, depending on the size of your quilt

Inserted strips: Leftover 1" strips of fabrics used in stars or other fabrics

Cutting

Instructions are for one inserted strip block.

Background: Cut 1 square 7" x 7".
Strips for Inserts: Cut strips 1" x 7" (or longer).

Making the Block

1. Using your straight-edge and rotary cutter, cut across the square at a slight angle. Don't measure; just cut the square into 2 pieces.

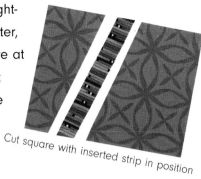
Cut square with inserted strip in position

2. With right sides together, sew a 1" strip to 1 side of the square, using a ¼" seam allowance. Sew the strip to the remaining side of the square. The square will maintain its original size if your inserted strip is 1" wide and you use ¼" seam allowances.

Block with one inserted strip

3. Press the seams toward the center of the strip. This gives it body.

4. Repeat Step 1, but this time make a cut that either intersects or runs alongside the existing strip. It's usually more effective if the inserted strips are not exactly parallel but random, moving in the same general direction.

Cut the square again.

5. Sew the pieces together as in Step 1. Press the seams toward the center of the strip.

6. Trim to a 6½" x 6½" block.

Block with two inserted strips

Putting It All Together

A sample layout is provided, but there is no set formula for putting your quilt together. This is when you design the quilt you want to make. Remember, there is no right or wrong way to put the quilt together. The fabrics and mood you select help express your individuality; now you compose the quilt.

Sample quilt layout

Begin by putting some star blocks on your design wall. Your first decision is whether you want your squares in horizontal rows or on point. I almost always work on a diagonal, setting the blocks on point because I think it is a more interesting layout. You also may want to offset the blocks.

Place the star blocks in groupings on the design wall, with maybe two or three in a cluster. Use transition blocks in the spaces between the star blocks. Begin making Inserted Strip blocks and add them to the wall in a random fashion between the star blocks. In some places you might leave two spaces between star blocks and fill the spots with a 6½" x 12½" rectangle. (Remember that everything is based on a 6" x 6" finished square.) The rectangle could contain one or more inserted strips. Try to vary the placement of strips in the different squares. I find it's usually best to keep the majority of the strips headed in the same general direction to give the feeling of motion, not confusion. Remember it's also important to have some strips appear to trail onto and off the edges of the quilt.

Continue to study what you have on your design wall; you will get a feel for whether the quilt needs more star or more transition blocks. Look for places where you need to add more space to give the quilt a more open feeling. Remember to include some transition blocks of plain background fabric without inserted strips, or with one strip barely showing. Some strips may blend in and some may be much stronger. You want the strips to enhance the focus blocks but not take over.

Blocks lined up square

Blocks on the diagonal

Blocks offset on the diagonal

Notice the variations on strip placement in the sample quilt. Some strips cross, others are close together. Some strips can also be pieced if you choose.

Continue adding and moving blocks until you are satisfied with your design. Your blocks are ready to be sewn together and the quilt completed. You may find that you have blocks left over. That's great! You have a head start on your next quilt.

Untitled
Sandi Cummings
48" x 48".

Tip: If you have a digital or Polaroid camera, take photos as you move the blocks around on the design wall and come up with combinations that feel right. Then you can continue to experiment with placement, yet find your way back to one of the original arrangements. I've never gone back to my original layout, but psychologically a photo frees me up to move blocks around. A quick picture also shows you where there is a problem with value and contrast, and helps identify areas where they need strengthening.

Stretching Exercise

Try making a quilt using just inserted strip transition blocks. This type of design, as in my *Carousel* quilt, makes a very dynamic, lively piece. The blocks need to be larger than you were working on before, perhaps 9" or 10". Notice the importance of value in this composition. It helps to have some value differences in the background fabric to add depth and a feeling of space and motion. Remember to leave areas without strips to provide resting spaces in the design. Too many strips give an overly busy, frenetic feel.

Carousel, Sandi Cummings, 46" x 40", quilted by Sandy Klop, corporate collection. This quilt is a good study in value. It needed the addition of the vertical strips to give it light. Photo by Joseph Untalan

Quilt detail using strip insertions
to add interest and connect units

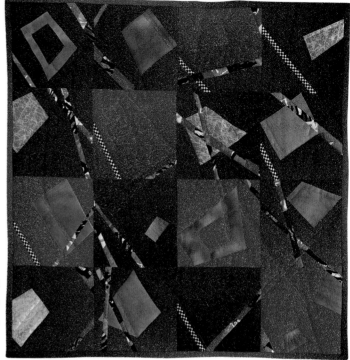

Surf's Up
Karen Flamme
32" x 32".

Eli's Quilt

Nancy Taylor
64" x 76"
Nancy has used strip insertions in
her quilts for years. This is a quilt
she made for her grandson, Eli.

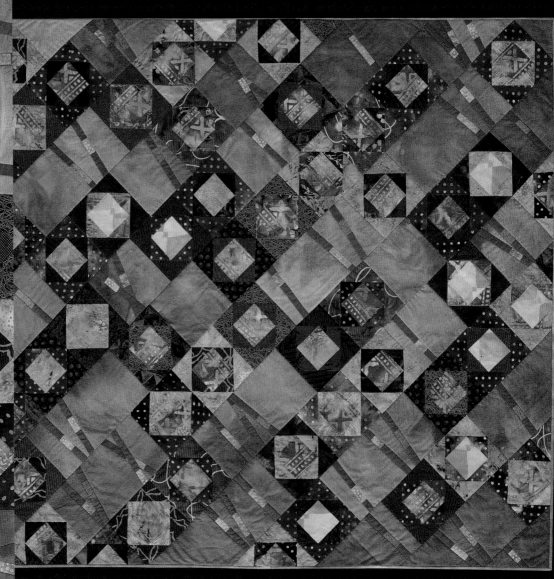

beyond the star

Sunrise, Sandi Cummings, 57" x 53".

Let's branch out a bit and move beyond the basic Star block. Other traditional blocks, such as Square-Within-a-Square, can be used successfully in place of the star in the quilt you just created. The 6" x 6" square format is a great way to try other traditional or original blocks with transition blocks. Freeform units can be used to substitute for star blocks.

Transition Blocks

There are many ways to use these blocks as connectors. Take a look at some of the photos in this book for ideas and inspiration. Then begin experimenting with the blocks on your design wall. The blocks may be set at an angle, staggered, or connected with various transition blocks. You won't be following any rules. As you play, you will discover combinations that please you and develop your personal style at the same time.

Trust Your Creativity

At this point you may feel a little unsettled because you're not following a strict pattern, and don't know just what your finished quilt is going to look like. Don't try to plan the quilt in advance. That's the fun of this style of quiltmaking. It leads to quilts full of lively spontaneity and your personality. The secret to designing as you go is to remain flexible and open to the possibilities that come to mind as your quilt develops. Don't worry, in time your creativity will evolve and take over as you experiment, and your confidence will gradually increase. Trust in yourself and your creativity!

6" Square-Within-a-Square Blocks

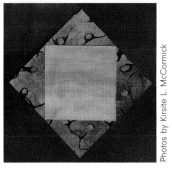

Photos by Kirsite L. McCormick

Beyond the Star

Fabric Requirements

Blocks: ¼ yard of at least 10-15 fabrics to get started. Each block uses 3 different fabrics. It is difficult to specify definite yardages because the size of the finished quilt is up to you. Include lights, mediums, and darks in a varying range of scale (see page 20). There should be an obvious value change between the squares within the block. I have boxes of leftover squares and scraps that I often dig into for a quilt such as this.

In the process of making blocks, you will no doubt "waste" some fabric, but I hope you choose fabrics you really like so there is a better chance you will love the quilt when you are finished. Think about mood and value as you choose your fabrics.

Cutting

Instructions are for one Square-Within-a-Square block.

Center square: Cut 1 square 3½" x 3½".

Middle square triangles: Cut 2 squares 3" x 3", then cut the squares diagonally into 4 triangles.

Outer square triangles: Cut 2 squares 3⅞" x 3⅞", then cut the squares diagonally into 4 triangles.

Making the Block

1. With right sides together, sew the triangles in pairs to the opposite sides of the center square, using ¼" seams and trying to match the points of the triangles.

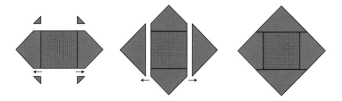

2. As in Step 1, sew the outer triangles to the center square.

Putting It All Together

Audition several different fabrics for your transition squares. I think of these squares as background, so I place the fabrics on my wall one at a time with the featured squares on top. Using your chosen fabric, make inserted strip transition blocks following the directions on page 27.

Try placing the blocks on your design wall on point, with the edges lined up evenly, or offset them. Play with the placement of the featured and transition blocks, but leave some background blocks plain or very simple. Notice how the focus squares play off the background, and pay particular attention to the distribution of value and scale throughout the quilt.

Freeform Units With Inserted Strips

These original 6" blocks are created without a template. They are easy-to-make freeform units that derive their personality from interesting centers and dynamic fabric combinations.

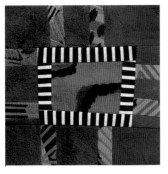

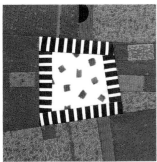

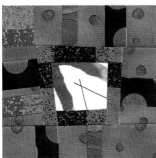

Fabric Requirements

Blocks: scraps of 4 different fabrics with fairly high contrast for each block

Cutting

Center: Using a straightedge and rotary cutter, cut an irregular square at a slight diagonal that is approximately 2½"–3" across.

Cut an irregular square.

Inside border: Cut 1 strip 1" x at least 18".
Outside border: Cut a 7" x 10" rectangle.
Inserted strips: Cut 2 strips 1" x at least 11".

Making the Block

1. Sew the 1"-wide inside border strip to 1 side of the center, using a ¼" seam allowance. Press the seam toward the strip. Trim the ends using the sides of the center as a guide. Repeat the process with the opposite side and then the 2 remaining sides. The original irregular shape now is bordered with 1" strips.

Strips added to the center

2. Now prepare a second, larger border with inserted strips. Use your ruler to make 2 lengthwise, slightly angled cuts through the 7" x 10" rectangle (along the 10" length). Insert the 1" strips using a ¼" seam allowance. Press seam allowances toward the strips. You now have a rectangle with inserted strips.

3. Cut the rectangle across the strips into four 2½" x 7" pieces.

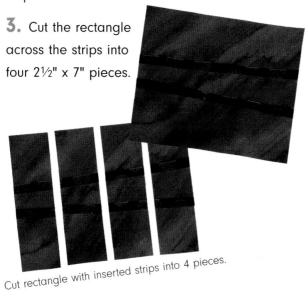

Cut rectangle with inserted strips into 4 pieces.

4. Join these pieces to the irregular square following Step 1. Press seams and trim edges so the square measures 6½" x 6½".

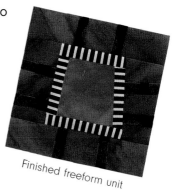

Finished freeform unit

Tip: When quilting this type of piece, I usually stitch in-the-ditch and don't do too much quilting. It's very effective to echo the strips in the transition blocks in blank areas where you feel more quilting is needed.

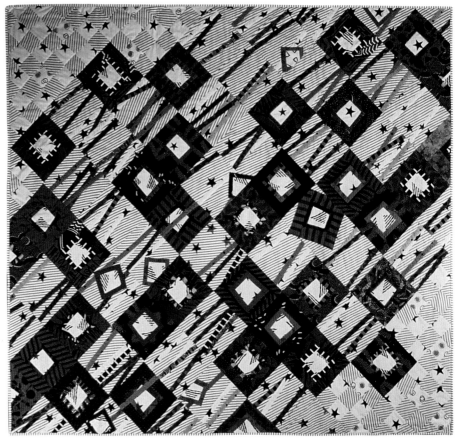

Family Ties Intermezzo
Sandi Cummings
52" x 48", quilted by Sandy Klop, private collection.
Photo by Joseph Untalan

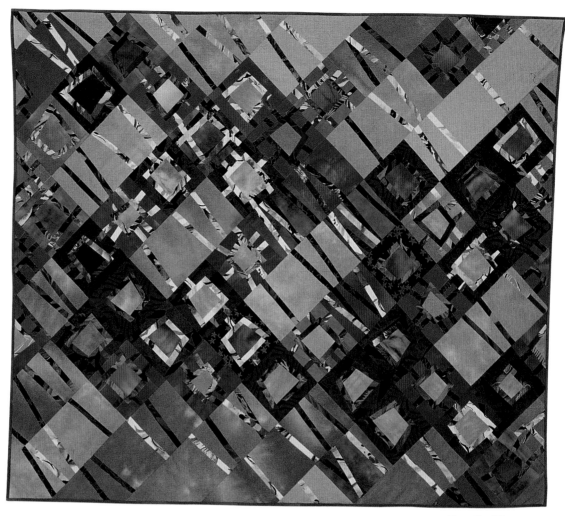

Family Ties

Sandi Cummings

52" x 48", quilted by Sandy Klop

corporate collection.

Photo by Joseph Untalan

Family Ties: Rhapsody

Sandi Cummings

61" x 55", quilted by Sandi Klop.

These units have an additional border
with strip insertions. Notice the cut corners
with checkerboard inserts.

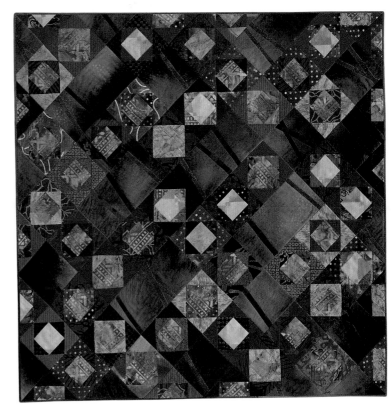

Sunset
Sandi Cummings
49" x 49".

Color Block 2: Mardi Gras
Brenda Smith
47" x 57".

Shards 9-1-1
Nina Shortridge
51" x 37".

double
your fun

Playtime, Sandi Cummings, 43" x 51".

You may already be familiar with cutting double. The basic technique is simple, but can lead to improvisation that results in a more complex block. Use variations of cutting double to make transition blocks or entire quilts, such as the Cutting Double Baby Quilt project that follows.

To begin, two squares are layered, then cut freestyle through both thicknesses. The pieces are alternated, reassembled, and sewn together to create two new pieced squares. The new squares are stacked on top of each other and the cutting and rearranging is repeated.

It may sound complicated, but it isn't. In fact, explaining the process to someone is harder than doing it! The fun of cutting double is the element of surprise. You don't have total control over the outcome, but new possibilities lead to results that are often better than you could have imagined or planned.

Our Cutting Double Baby Quilt project is made entirely of double-cut squares. It's a very fast, fun, and easy quilt to make. Once you are comfortable with cutting double, there are plenty of variations to play with: inserted strips, irregular checkerboards, double X's, and pieced checkerboards. These help get you started with experimenting on your own.

Cutting Double Baby Quilt

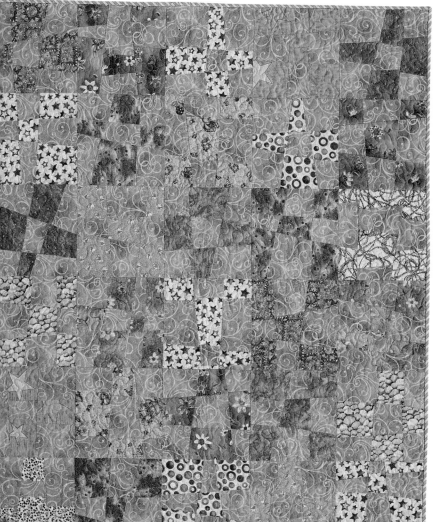

> **Finished Size:** 35½" x 42½"
> **Finished Block Size:** 7"

Fabric Requirements
The background fabric is used in every square; choose other fabrics to complement it.

Background fabric: 1¼ yards
Blocks: 15 squares at least 10" x 10" from a variety of contrasting but complementary fabrics
Binding: ⅝ yard
Batting: 40" x 47"
Backing: 1⅓ yards

Cutting

Background: Cut 15 squares 10" x 10".
Contrast fabrics: Cut 15 squares 10" x 10".

Making the Blocks

1. Place 1 background square right side up on your cutting mat. Layer a contrasting square right side up on top of the background square.

2. Make 2 freehand vertical cuts through both layers. The cuts may be straight or slightly curved. I want to emphasize *slightly* curved; if you make an "S" curve this method will not work. Don't make the space between the cuts too narrow since they have to include seam allowances. Make your cuts straight or curved, but stick with 1 type of cut throughout the quilt so it doesn't look too chaotic. Vary the placement of the cuts so the blocks all look different. For the Cutting Double Baby Quilt all of the cuts are straight, but were made without a ruler.

Pieces laid out for Cutting Double squares

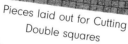

Cut the stacked fabric.

3. Separate the 2 layers, alternating the pieces as you lay them out into 2 new squares.

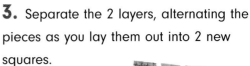

Reassemble the pieces for 2 blocks.

4. Sew the pieces together using ¼" seam allowances. Press the seams flat; there is no need to clip the curves.

Tip: If the cuts are curved it is important to sew the seams with a scant ¼" seam allowance so they don't pucker.

Tip: When sewing gentle curves, keep in mind that in some spots you are dealing with bias edges. Don't tug on these edges as you sew or they may not lie flat. Line the 2 fabrics up with right sides together as usual, and gently hold them together as you sew a couple of inches, reposition your hold, and sew a few more inches until you have finished your seam. Make the seam allowances a scant ¼". In these blocks the bottoms of the seamlines will probably not match up.

5. Layer the 2 new squares with right sides up so the seams are vertical. For a different look you can rotate 1 of the squares 180° so the cuts remain vertical, but not identical. Make 2 free-hand horizontal cuts— either straight or slightly curved, depending on what you started with— through both layers.

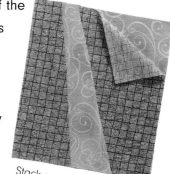

Stack squares right sides up with seams in a vertical position.

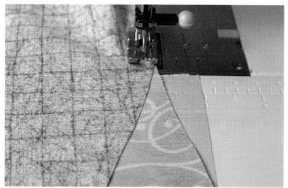

Position curves to sew.

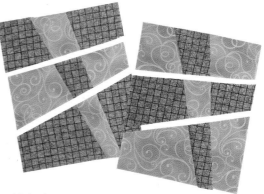

Make horizontal cuts and reassemble new squares.

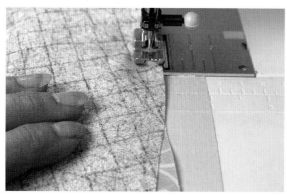

Sew a few inches at a time.

6. Reassemble the squares, alternating the fabrics as you did before. Sew these new squares together. Line the pieces up at the top when you start sewing them, but don't try to match seams or the bottom edges of the squares. The great thing about this technique is that nothing has to match!

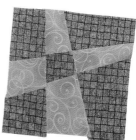

Finished squares

7. Trim each square to 7½" x 7½".

8. Place the blocks on your design wall in random order in a 5 block x 6 block setting. Step back and study your arrangement. Move the blocks around until you have a combination of pattern, color, and contrast that is pleasing to you. That's it!

9. Sew the blocks together to complete your quilt top.

10. Layer, baste, quilt, and bind your quilt using your preferred technique.

Block Variations

Make Three Cuts

Follow Steps 1–4 for the first set of cuts and reassembly. Layer the 2 new squares so the seams are vertical. This time make 3 horizontal cuts instead of 2. Alternate the fabric pieces as before, and sew the squares together. Keep in mind that 3 cuts will make your square smaller than 2 cuts because there are more seams. A 10" x 10" block is large enough to accommodate 3 cuts, and will result in a finished 7½" x 7½" block. Square up the blocks and finish the quilt.

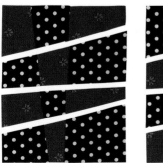
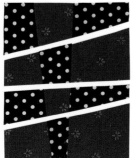

Blocks with 3 cuts

Reverse Blocks

Follow Steps 1–4, except make the cuts to the far left or far right. Turn 1 of the blocks 180° (all the cuts run in a vertical direction). Stack the blocks and make horizontal cuts. This time make a very wide angled cut. Proceed as before.

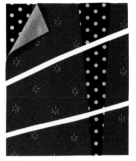

Cutting for Reverse blocks

Completed Reverse blocks

Use More than Two Layers of Fabric

Stack more than 2 layers of fabric to start. Cut through all thicknesses, then begin alternating pieces to reassemble the squares. Sew the pieces together.

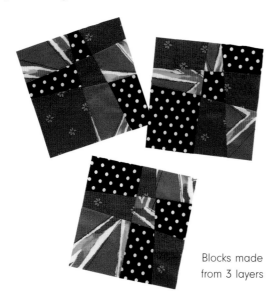

Blocks made from 3 layers

Tip: The size of the finished square depends on how many cuts you make. The more cuts you make, the smaller the piece gets due to the seams. If you want to make a lot of cuts, you will have to use much larger blocks to begin with. Try to vary the cuts from narrow to wide, but keep in mind that if the cut is too narrow it will disappear into the seam allowance. Remember that you don't have to cut every block every time.

Cutting Double with Inserted Strips

This block combines techniques from the Inserted Strip block on page 27 and the Cutting Double Baby Quilt on page 40.

Fabric Requirements

Block: pieces at least 10" x 10" of 2 contrasting fabrics

Inserted strips: scraps at least 1" x 12" of a variety of fabrics

Cutting

Block: Cut 1 square 10" x 10" from each of 2 contrasting fabrics.

Inserted strips: Cut 2 or 3 strips 1" x at least 12" from a variety of fabrics.

Making the Block

1. Place 1 square right side up on the cutting mat. Layer a contrasting square right side up on top.

2. Make 2 freehand vertical cuts through both layers. The cuts may be straight or slightly curved. Don't make the cuts too narrow because they need to include the seam allowance.

3. Separate the 2 layers, alternating the pieces as you lay them out into 2 new squares.

New squares

4. Sew the pieces together using ¼" seam allowances to make 2 new squares. Press the seams flat.

5. Layer the 2 new squares on top of each other, right sides up with the seams vertical. Make 1 freehand horizontal cut, either straight or slightly curved, through both layers.

6. Separate 1 piece from 1 layer of the cut square. (I usually use 1 of the larger pieces). Make 2 or 3 cuts perpendicular to the original cut. Now add 1" strips between the pieces, following the instructions from the Inserted Strip block (page 27).

Insert strips in 1 piece
of 1 layer.

7. Place this new unit back in its original position, then make a second cut through both layers, perpendicular to the inserted strips.

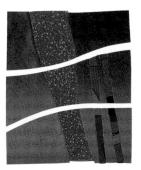

Cut both layers.

8. Reassemble the squares, alternating the pieces as before. Sew the pieces together using ¼" seam allowances to make 2 new squares. (If your cuts are curved it is important that the seams are scant.) The bottoms of your seamlines will probably not match; don't worry about it. Press seams flat using steam; it is not necessary to clip the curves.

9. Square up each block.

Cutting Double
Gallery

Zen Pathways
Ginny Cooke
32" x 32".
This quilt shows many
variations of cutting double.

Tropical Rain Forest
Sandi Cummings
35" x 35", corporate collection.

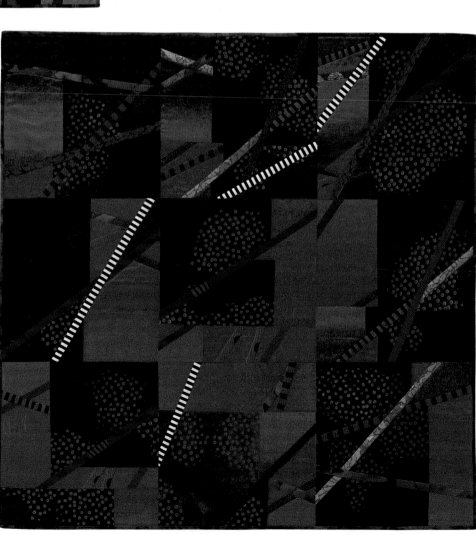

Searching for the Light

Marilyn Felber

41" x 57".

Marilyn combined cutting double blocks with pieced
blocks to create a complex design.

Winter Light

Sandi Cummings

50" x 33", corporate collection.

Morning Light

Sandi Cummings

30" x 30".

Untitled

Sandi Cummings

21" x 21", corporate collection.

Photo by Sandi Cummings

Connections

Marcia Stein

42" x 42".

Photo by Marcia Stein

Kelp Forest II
Sandi Cummings
46" x 54", corporate collection.

Photo by Don Tuttle

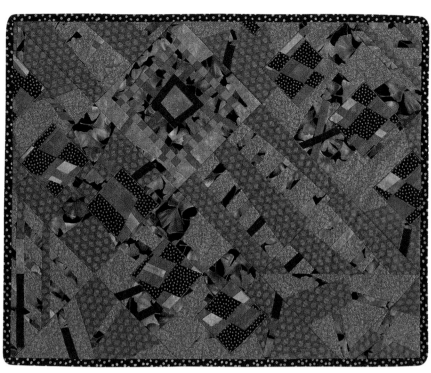

Key Lime
Ginny Guffey
36" x 29".

Untitled

Karen Flamme

39" x 44".

This quilt features just three
fabrics and all straight cuts.

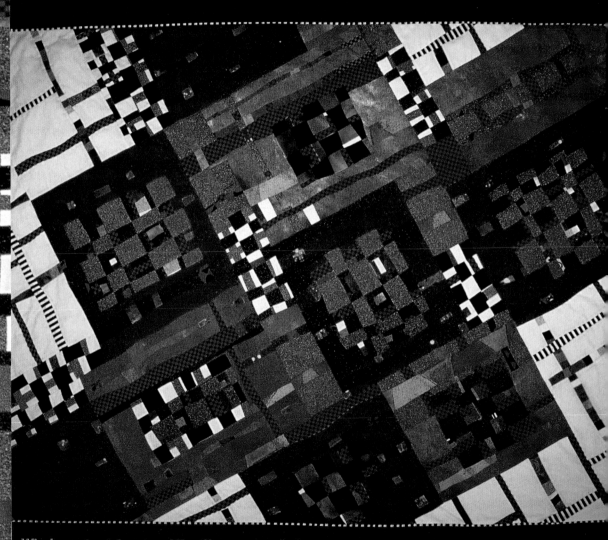

just keep
cutting double

Windows, Sandi Cummings, 58" x 48", corporate collection. Photo by Joseph Untalan

As you can see, cutting double is fast and fun, with surprising results that add interest and motion to your quilts. There are a few more cutting double variations that are wonderful as transition blocks, backgrounds, or borders. You might not want to make a whole quilt with them, but a few will add interesting light and contrast that can bring an otherwise flat area to life.

Irregular Checkerboard Blocks

Irregular Checkerboards are what they sound like: Irregular blocks of light and dark fabrics that play off each other. Pieced Irregular Checkerboards look more complex, but are easy to make. Cutting Double X's make a spectacular border for a quilt. The directions that follow lead you step-by-step, then you may want to begin experimenting on your own.

Irregular Checkerboards can be used as transition blocks.

Landscape VI
Sandi Cummings
45" x 45".
Sections of this quilt use the cutting-double method.
Photo by Don Tuttle

Fabric Requirements

Blocks: pieces at least 8" x 12" of 2 fabrics, 1 light and 1 dark

Cutting

Blocks: Cut an 8" x 12" rectangle of each fabric.

Making the Block

1. With right sides up, layer a dark and a light rectangle. Using a rotary cutter, but no straightedge, make vertical cuts through both layers, varying the width of the strips. Your strips need to include seam allowances, so don't cut them too narrow.

> Tip: When making an irregular checkerboard it is important to make it irregular *enough* so the viewer knows that it was intentional, rather than just careless cutting and sewing.

2. Alternating the strips from each fabric, arrange them into 2 sets. Use a ¼" seam allowance to sew the strips together.

Vertical strips sewn together

3. With right sides up, place the 2 sewn sets on top of each other. Make horizontal cuts, varying the width of the strips. Again, remember to make the strips wide enough to include a ¼" seam allowance.

4. Alternate the strips from each set to create a checkerboard effect.

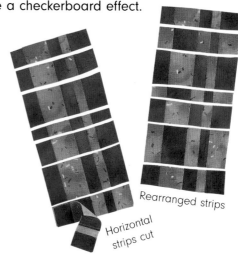

Rearranged strips

Horizontal strips cut

5. Sew the strips together to make 2 new Checkerboard blocks.

The completed Irregular Checkerboard block

> Tip: Irregular Checkerboards can also be made by layering 3 fabrics: 1 light, 1 medium, and 1 dark.

54

Cottages by the Sea II, Karen Flamme, 43" x 40".

Pieced Irregular Checkerboards

To make a pieced Irregular Checkerboard, start by piecing one of the fabrics—the dark or the light—before cutting double. Do not piece both; you will lose the checkerboard effect and it will become very confusing.

Fabric Requirements

Blocks: pieces of 2 fabrics, 1 light and 1 dark

Inserted strips: strips of several medium-range fabrics in varying widths, 1"–2" wide.

Preparing for Block Assembly

1. Cut a 10" x 10" square of the light fabric. You will insert strips into this square. Begin by making a freehand cut about a third of the way from 1 edge.

2. Insert a 2"-wide strip.

Cut piece with strip insert

3. Cut the square a third of the way over, across the inserted strip. Rotate 1 cut side 180° and insert another strip.

Rotated side with strip insert

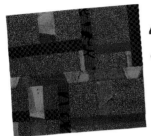

Piece with more cuts and strips

4. Make as many cuts and add as many strips as you choose.

Block Assembly

1. Cut a piece of dark fabric the same size as the pieced square. Put this right side up under the pieced square and make vertical cuts through both layers, varying the width of the strips.

Layer pieced and solid squares.

2. Alternating the strips from each fabric, arrange them in 2 sets. Sew the strips together. Press the seams to the right on 1 piece, and to the left on the other.

3. With rights sides up, place the 2 sewn sets on top of each other. This time make horizontal cuts, varying the width of the strips. Alternate the strips from each set to create a checkerboard effect.

4. Sew the strips together to make 2 new checkerboard squares.

5. Trim to the desired size.

Examples of completed blocks

Cutting Double X Blocks

This technique is especially effective as a border or in small sections of a quilt.

Fabric Requirements
Blocks: ⅓ yard of 1 light and 1 dark fabric

Cutting
Blocks: Cut 1 rectangle approximately 9" x 22" from each fabric. You will sew a lot of seams, so the final piece will be much narrower than 22". The top and bottom measurements (9") will not change much.

Making the Block
1. Layer 1 dark and 1 light rectangle with right sides up.

2. Use a rotary cutter to make diagonal cuts for 1 side of each X. Make all of these cuts in the same direction. Don't make the cuts too close together.

3. Alternating the strips from each fabric, rearrange them into 2 new sets.

4. Sew the sets together.

Make the first diagonal cuts, alternate pieces,
sew sets together, and layer.

Tip: Try adding rough-cut circles, either the same or different sizes, to both fabric squares (either plain or pieced) before cutting double. See *Royal Rags* on page 82.

5. With right sides again facing up, stack the 2 sewn sets on top of each other in their original positions. Make diagonal cuts in the opposite direction, crossing the seams from the first set of cuts.

Make the second diagonal cuts.

Squares before cutting double

Completed squares

6. Once again, alternate the strips from each set. Sew the strips together. If you make your cuts close together, they will overlap at the top and bottom. If the cuts are farther apart you will get simpler X's.

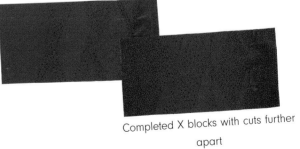

Completed X blocks with close cuts

Completed X blocks with cuts further apart

Chapter 8

bring your
garden inside

Garden Light, Sandi Cummings, 38" x 38", quilted by Sandy Klop, corporate collection. Photo by Sandi Cummings

Inspiration for my quilts comes from many different places: colors, photographs, interesting shapes, landscapes, or, in this case, the view from my studio window. The garden features a large hedge that is constantly changing, with values ranging from very dark to very light. In some of the shadowy areas the green leaves appear to be black, while in other areas where the sun hits the top of the leaves, the glare makes them look white. The contrasts and deep shadows change depending on the time of day and the seasons.

One day I took two fabrics that looked great together and started strip piecing them, not really knowing what was going to grow out of my efforts. After a while I realized that the view from my studio window was influencing my work. After years of staring into this space I realized there was a garden quilt waiting to be made.

Photos by Sandi Cummings

Garden Lattice quilts are strip-pieced creations that let you use your favorite large, clear, floral fabrics to achieve spectacular light and shadow effects.

For this project strips are sewn together to create new pieces of fabric. The new pieces are cut into triangles, then the triangles are arranged to suggest light filtering through foliage.

Creating a garden lattice quilt is a good exercise for experimenting with block placement on a design wall. You can turn pieces and move them around until you get just the look you want. I like to have all the strips placed in one direction with the light source coming from the opposite direction. I think it keeps your quilt from becoming too static, and it adds a feeling of depth.

Combinations of fabrics such as these work well for garden lattice quilts.

Garden Lattice Quilt

Fabric Requirements

Look for large, well-defined, clear florals. I prefer floral fabrics that are not too grayed, with flowers that don't have too many lines or shadows in them. It is also important to have dark, medium, and light fabrics, but most of the darks need some light in them and vice versa. If you look through a group of trees or bushes on a sunny day you will always see a sparkle of light; this is the effect you want to create.

Sometimes there is one color I'm not happy with in a fabric that I want to use. I cut the fabric into strips, cut out the unwanted color in a strip, then sew the strip back together. This can make it much easier to find fabrics suitable for Garden Lattice quilts.

Cut out unwanted color and re-sew the strip.

The required yardage depends on the size of your finished quilt. A piece of fabric 13" x 42" is enough for two sets of 10 strips. I sew a lot of strips together that are cut into triangles I never use because I don't like the end results. While I am making a quilt, I continually search for and add more fabrics.

When you sew strips together you are creating new fabric. When I work, I often keep the strips in order so the viewer sees the whole flower. Other times I mix them up, or turn the strips top to bottom. It depends on how I want to distribute the light or value in the strips, or how much of the original fabric pattern I want to show. I think about whether I want whole flowers in some areas.

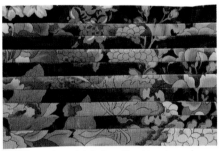

New pieced fabric with strips in order

New pieced fabric with strips flipped

As I compose a quilt I expect to have some fabric and triangles left over. Leftovers are good; you'll discover how to use them in Chapter 9.

Cutting

Cut 5 strips 1¼" x width of fabric of each of 2 fabrics.

Making the Blocks

1. Sew the 10 strips together lengthwise using a ¼" seam allowance, alternating the 2 fabrics so the lights and darks create a dappled effect. The new pieced fabric should be approximately 8" x 42".

2. Fold the new pieced fabric in half so it measures 8" x 21", and cut into mirror-image half-square triangles with 8" sides.

Cut mirror image triangles.   Triangles ready to assemble into square

3. Combine 4 triangles to form a block with the strips all going in the same direction. Place your triangles on your design wall right away to see what is happening. I often find surprises when I combine strips of 2 different fabrics. Are they looking the way you imagined? Do you like the effect? Is there enough light coming through?

4. Repeat Steps 1–3 using more fabric combinations. For some sets be sure to use 1 previously used fabric with a new fabric to provide a good transition. Within each set of 10 strips, choose pairs of strips that provide a good mix of darks, mediums, and lights.

5. Continue putting the triangles on your design wall. As you place the new blocks on the wall and begin to design your quilt, remember what a garden might look like. There are light, sunny areas and dark, shadowed areas. Move your triangles around on the wall to achieve the effect of light coming through the foliage.

Stand back and decide if you are creating the feeling you want. Do you need more dark or light areas? Make more triangles as needed. Watch your quilt garden grow as you add triangles and move them around until you are pleased with the results.

Sunbeams, Karen Flamme, 33" x 34". The triangles in this quilt are laid out horizontally.

Garden Corner

Sandi Cummings
36" x 36", quilted by Sandy
Klop, corporate collection.

Photo by Sandi Cummings

Garden Lattice IV
Sandi Cummings
64" x 54", quilted by Sandy Klop, corporate collection.
Photo by Joseph Untalan

Tip: When I'm nearing completion of a design, but before I start sewing it together, if I find that one particular triangle needs a little more value difference, I may go in and remove one of the strips in the triangle and replace it with another. Sometimes that bit of extra effort is what is necessary before sewing the blocks together.

Tip: Don't be afraid to experiment with the triangles on your design wall: turn the pieces and move them around. Take a digital or Polaroid photo when you have a design you like. It can help you zero in on any value problems. A photo also allows you to confidently move blocks around because you will be able to get back to where you started.

Checkerboard Lattice
Sandi Cummings
33" x 34".

Photo by Joseph Untalan

everybody

ves leftovers

Leftovers are great because they give you a head start on your next quilt. You don't have to select and shop for ingredients (in this case fabric!), you can just make things up as you go along, and there are no instructions to follow.

I always have trouble throwing out the leftover scraps right after I complete a quilt, so I bag them up in a clear plastic bag and throw them into a big box. One group of tag ends was so beautiful I felt like I wanted to do something with it right away. That evening I started cutting the scraps freehand and sewing them into small units, and that's how my love for leftovers began.

Now that you have completed many of the projects in this book, you no doubt have plenty of leftover fabric scraps: cut-off corners, leftover strips, and odd-shaped pieces. These leftovers are pieced together in random order, then squared-off, and a wide, frame-like border is attached. The result is a small design study, full of detail and interest.

Leftover Size

The finished size is totally arbitrary. If I am making a grouping of leftover pieces, I like to keep the outside dimensions the same and the centers fairly close in size: approximately 8" x 10" or 9" x 12".

I think of these creations as small compositions with the border as an integral part of the design, serving as the mat and complimenting the center. Making leftovers is a relaxing way to end the day. You can play with scraps when you are tired and don't want to think about following instructions or being precise.

Untitled, Sandi Cummings, 15" x 13", corporate collection. Photo by Kate Cameron

Everybody Loves Leftovers

Fabric Requirements

Blocks: scraps

Border: if you don't use scraps, ¼ yard should be plenty, depending on the size of your project.

Buckram* or stiff interfacing: the size of your finished piece, including the border

Batting: the size of your finished piece, including the border

Backing: the size of your finished piece, including the border

Strips of fusible web and a sheet of fusible web the size of your finished piece

*Buckram is a coarse cotton fabric sized with glue and is used as an interlining or interfacing. We use it to stiffen small quilts. It is available in apparel fabric stores and is sold by the yard.

Making the Sections

Select a bag of scraps you would like to work with. Sort out any interesting pieces you particularly like. Since you've already used these fabrics successfully in a quilt, you know they work well together. Feel free to add other fabrics as you proceed, although that will probably not be necessary.

Begin by cutting triangles freehand and combining them to make "squares." Calling them "squares" is questionable since they will be lopsided and irregular. Some will also be bigger than others, but that doesn't matter. The size should vary from about ½" to 2", but scale may be determined by how detailed you want your piece to be. You might also make fused or pieced stars, bars, or four-patches. The combinations are unlimited. Remember that the goal is to have each little square or element pleasing in itself.

At this point don't worry about where they will go. Use a small seam allowance, about ⅛", or whatever is comfortable, since you are working with such small pieces.

After you have made many of the little "squares" or combinations, try putting some of them together to make larger units. Combine horizontal, vertical, and diagonal elements and try to vary your placement. The "squares," for example, can be in a straight row, a pinwheel, on point, horizontal, and so on. If something is too small, add a strip to make it the right size and to add interest. Remember this is freeform and spontaneous.

Next, start putting the units on your design wall. Move them around, rearrange them, and make some combinations that you think are interesting. Stand back to see how these read from a distance, but you don't need to go across the room. These are smaller, more intimate pieces of art. The viewer will come close to see them.

When you like what you have and there are enough units to fill about three-quarters of the finished size, start making elements to connect everything or to balance things out. Usually it is more of the same.

Alternatives

An alternative design method is to work in the familiar square format and make your units 3" x 3" squares. Join these squares together and finish with a border.

Making the Border

Remember that the piece doesn't have to be squared off; the edges can be uneven. When you are satisfied with your composition you are ready to design a border. The border is important, as a good one will really enhance the center.

Your border can be all one fabric or a combination of fabrics. If the border is pieced there should be less value difference in the pieces than in the center. A border should complement the center rather than compete with it.

Untitled, Sandi Cummings, 15" x 13" corporate collection. Photo by Kate Cameron

A fairly wide border seems to work better than a narrow one. Think of it as a mat around a small painting.

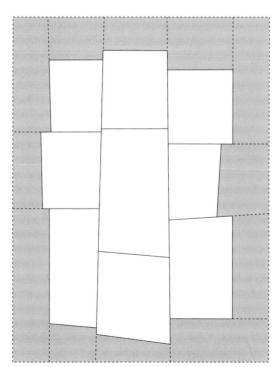

Attach borders to sections.

Cut the border strips a generous 1" larger all the way around than you want the finished piece to be. Sew the border strips to the center section. If your sections are different sizes and the outside edges of the center section are uneven, attach the border strips to the sections before you sew them together.

Finishing

1. Cut pieces of buckram (or stiff interfacing) and batting the same size you would like your finished, bordered piece to be when completed.

2. Machine baste the batting to the buckram with a large stitch. Sometimes ironing the 2 together will make it hold in place, but that usually only works for a cotton batting.

3. Layer the following on a worktable: buckram, batting, and finished top right side up.

4. Quilting: I usually do very little quilting on these pieces, as I don't think they really need it.

5. Turn the edges of the border to the back and use strips of fusible web to adhere the borders to the back of the buckram.

6. Fuse adhesive web to a piece of backing fabric. Cut backing fabric 1" smaller than the finished size.

7. Center the backing fabric on top of the turned edges of the border and iron securely in place.

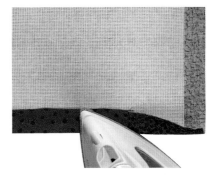

Edges of border turned to back

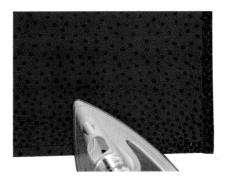

Center backing fabric

Karen Flamme, 12" x 12"

Karen Flamme, 12" x 12"

Gallery of Leftovers

15" x 15"

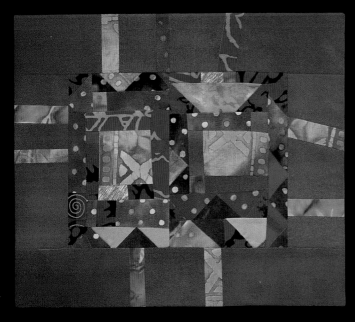

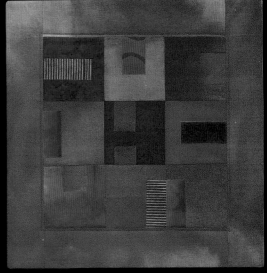

Sandi Cummings
15" x 15"

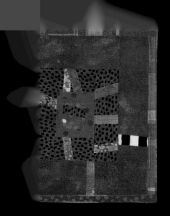
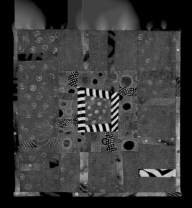
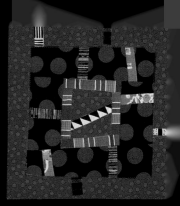

Peggy McKay Termir
12" x 12

Sandi Cummings
15" x 13"

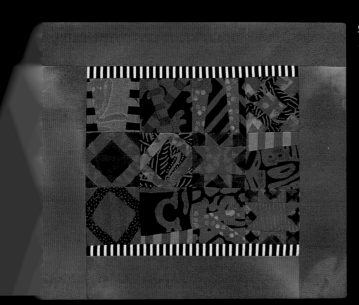

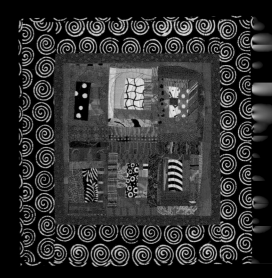

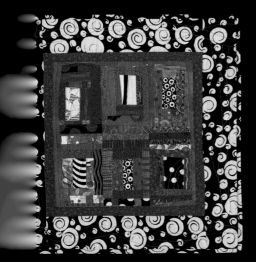

y McKay Termini
20"

Chapter 10

Compose
your own quilts

As you've completed the projects you have learned to make a variety of units and put them together into quilts. Now it's time for you to experiment on your own: make more units, play with them on your design wall, and create your own composition. After all, that's what this style of quilting is all about: playing with fabric, trying new things, being flexible and open to surprises, having fun, and expressing your own creativity.

Jump Right In

How should you get started? Often I begin with a basic idea in mind, but no clear vision of the finished piece. I start by deciding on a method of construction, then I assemble an array of fabrics. I frequently use the block format, and some of the units you've learned in the projects, because it gives me a structure around which to work. I make blocks or units, and as the piece progresses, I become more concerned about the design of the quilt as a whole. For me, it seems more manageable to work this way than to plan the entire quilt out in advance. I try to be open to what is happening with the piece as I work. If a small area is particularly exciting and triggers another idea, I will drop my original concept and take off in a different direction. You'll find that when you are experimenting, things do not always go as planned.

One reason I like to work this way is that there is always the chance that exciting unplanned relationships will emerge in the quilt. The results may be far from what I originally envisioned and there are often happy surprises.

Begin by making some units. Don't worry at this point about them being too dark or too light, too busy or too plain. Just make some things that are pleasing to you and put them up on your design wall. If some look too dark, you can make some lighter units. If they look too busy, you can make some plainer ones to add to the mix. If something looks particularly good, try repeating it, perhaps with a slight variation. Add these new units to your first group. Now, when you view them all together you can begin to get more critical and decide what you want to add and where to go from there.

The contrast between setting blocks straight or on the diagonal is dramatic in this example.

73

Critiquing Your Design

I'm usually very happy at this point. I'm enthusiastic and surprised at how well things are going. I am filled with optimism. However, when things are nearing completion I may have doubts and begin questioning the design decisions I made along the way, since I have not been working from a pre-planned pattern. This is when I need to leave my intuitive self behind and make an effort to pull out my bag of tools. I ask questions that help move me toward a more critical, rational, or left-brain approach, such as the following:

Tip: As you put units up on your design wall, put them close together so no white shows around them. There will not be white space in the finished quilt, and its presence will be deceptive in analyzing value.

Value: Are there enough lights, mediums, and darks?

Balance: Is there equal distribution of visual weight in the design?

Are the color, value, and texture balanced?

Scale: Is there enough variety?

Mood: Do all the components speak to the mood I am trying to create?

Focus: Is there a focus? Do I want one? Are there resting spots?

Unity: Are the various elements well connected? Is there anything I can do to help tie things together? Would connecting strips or transition blocks help?

I use this checklist so I can remain objective about my own work, then brainstorm to come up with viable solutions. I ask, "What if I try this?" or "What if I try that?" This is a good time for experimentation; I focus on the strongest idea and go with it. I need to be willing to waste time and fabric and try new ideas.

Dealing with Quilter's Block

If you get stuck and don't know how to keep going, don't worry; this is the point when usually you'll start coming up with your best solutions. Use "being stuck" as a turning point to being inventive and creative. I use this opportunity to contemplate how I can make my quilt interesting and unique. Think about the quilts you have made that you like. Do any of them have successful elements in them that you can apply to this quilt? Sometimes it helps to leave the pieces on your design wall for a while and let ideas simmer. Other times it's better to put a quilt away for a little while, then take it out and look at it with fresh eyes.

Sometimes I get stuck simply because I'm spending too much time thinking about the design and over-analyzing solutions rather than just working. When that happens I make myself get to work and fill in the blank spaces to finish the quilt. Once there is something on the wall I can usually see what needs to be done.

Don't Stop Now

What size do you want your quilt to be? Many of my quilts are large because they seem to carry more impact that way. I frequently tell my students to keep working and make the quilt larger. I think there is a tendency to stop too soon. Ask yourself if the addition of more blocks will improve the quilt and its impact. Are there some variations on your theme that you would like to include? Don't stop just to have it finished.

When nearing completion of a quilt I often take a break to tidy things up on the design wall. I stand back to study what's going on, and often cut strips from a roll of white paper. I pin these on the sides of the quilt to mask off the ragged edges. This gives me a good idea of what the finished piece will look like. The rough edges and extra fabric can be very distracting.

A Question of Borders

Think about whether the quilt needs borders. While they can be effective, I don't often add borders because they tend to close things in.

Audition a potential border fabric by pinning it on your design wall. Place the quilt on top of the fabric with just the planned amount of border showing. I try to use a fabric close in value to the quilt top because I think the borders should be an integral part of the quilt rather than a frame around it. I often insert elements such as strips or checkerboards to help integrate the border. Bindings should be an integral part of the quilt; I use a fabric close in value to the body of the quilt. If it is a high-contrast quilt I use a medium value.

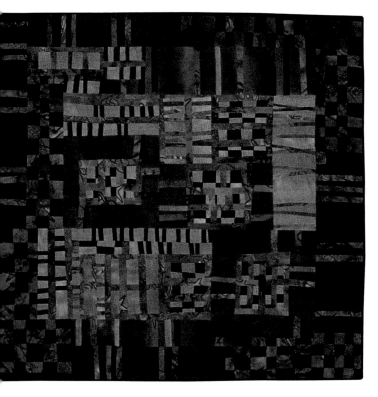

As you solve design issues and find ways to fix problem areas, you are developing your personal style. Just as a music composer will return again and again to certain components, you, as a visual artist, will discover you rely on various elements to complete your work or reflect your taste. In this way your personal style evolves.

Penthouse, Sandi Cummings, 39" x 42", quilted by Sandy Klop, corporate collection. The checkerboards and inserted strips were added to the border to help soften and integrate it into the quilt.

Here are some ways to generate ideas and help you identify your own personal taste.

- **Attend art exhibitions** as often as possible.

- Always **carry a camera.**

- **Collect pictures** that you like from magazines, newspapers, and other sources.

- Take photos inside and around the outside of your home. **Photograph things** that have interesting line and design elements. Notice how shadow and light change throughout the day. This helps you become more aware of your environment.

- When you **walk into a gallery** or room in a museum, notice which pieces you are drawn to. What was it that attracted you to them? Are they your favorites when you leave?

- **When you see a painting** or any piece of artwork, **stop** and try to figure out what makes that piece of art either successful or not.

- When you walk into a room that you like, stop and **think about** what makes it so appealing. Is it the **colors, use of light,** placement of furniture, objects of art?

- **Work in a series** (more on that in the next chapter).

- **Fold your fabric** and really look at each piece.

Gallery of
Creative Results

Bicentennial

Sandi Cummings

72" x 52".

I liked the idea of combining the traditional pieced stars with the more contemporary design features of this quilt. The traditional star blocks add to a "down home" feel, while the background with its floating circles and squares lends a more fanciful feeling. I attempted to create a magical quality in this quilt.

Photo by Don Tuttle

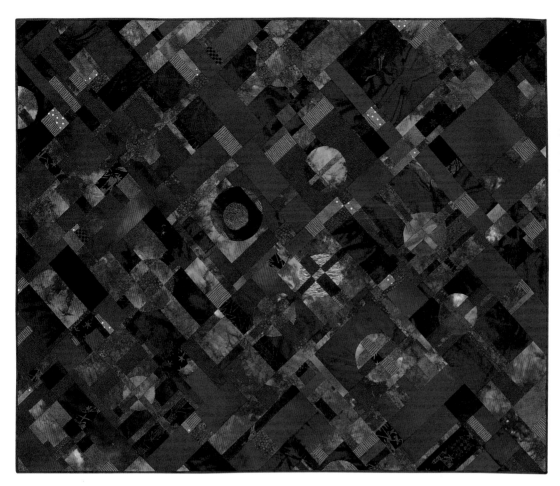

Crop Circles,
Sandi Cummings,
57" x 46", corporate
collection.
Photo by Don Tuttle

**Not My
Grandma's Quilt**
Jo Anne Parkin
42" x 33"
Jo Anne used cutting
double and inserted strips,
among other techniques,
to create an energetic
and lively quilt.

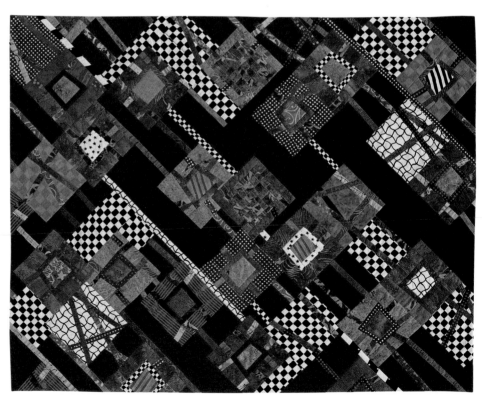

Ladies of the Day

Sandi Cummings

70" x 65"

The unusual figures established the mood of the quilt and influenced the fabrics I chose for their setting. The entire background is made by cutting double.

Photo by Don Tuttle

1997

Sandi Cummings

96" x 78", corporate collection.

Pieced fabric seemed to take away from the impact of the women, so in the foreground and upper background I inserted patterned fabric between the batting and quilt top and held it in place with quilting stitches. The pattern lightly shows through to add depth. I think this quilt reflects the power and endurance that women are beginning to claim for themselves today.

Photo by Don Tuttle

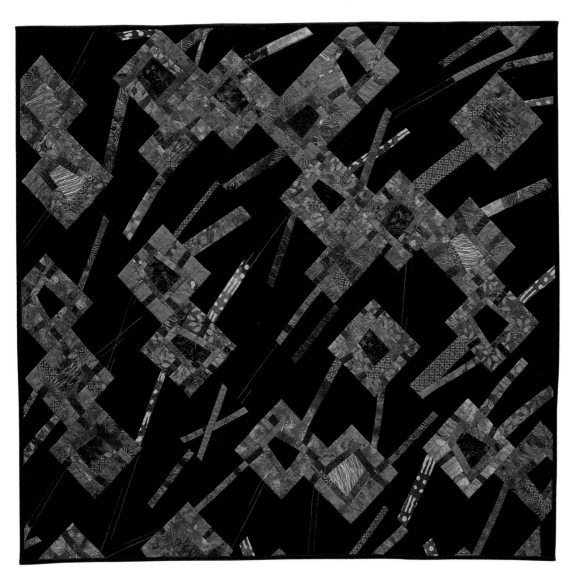

Northern Lights

Karen Flamme
48" x 45".
The pieced blocks in this quilt are enhanced by the inserted strips, which give the blocks a feeling of motion and energy.

Cold Winter Quilt

Sandi Cummings
50" x 44", collection of Nina Shortridge.
The cutting double technique was used in several places in this piece. This quilt is one of a series of landscape quilts.

Photo by Don Tuttle

Royal Rags

Sandi Cummings

52" x 68", corporate collection.

The richness of the fabric set the mood for this
quilt and demanded a quiet balance between
complexity and simplicity. It would have been
difficult, if not impossible, to make this quilt
without using the cutting double method.

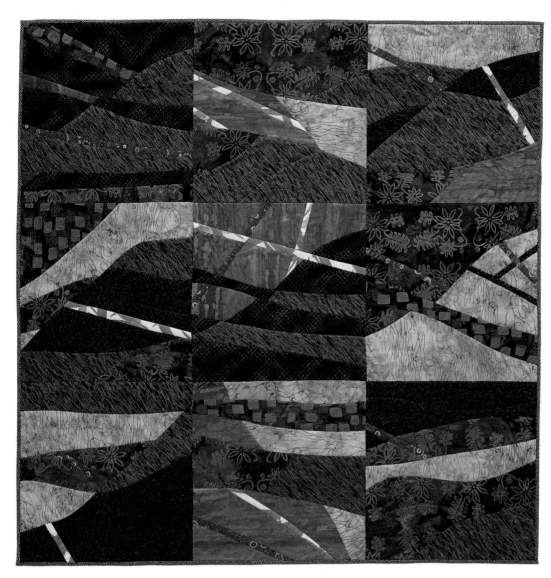

Crossroads

Karen Flamme
50" x 50".
Karen applied double cutting through several layers and inserted strips to create a strong, yet restful landscape.

Garden Lattice VI

Sandi Cummings
64" x 54", quilted by Sandy Klop, corporate collection.
This quilt was a lesson in patience. The color combinations are so unusual that it took me almost a year to find the right fabrics to complete it.

Photo by Joseph Untalan

you did it once,
now do it again

Worlds Apart II, Sandi Cummings, 54" x 54", corporate collection. Photo by Don Tuttle

Work in a Series

Working in a series is a good way to jump into making a quilt without first having to agonize over basic structure and design. It also gives credence to the old adage "practice makes perfect," or, if not perfect, at least easier and more interesting. You're not copying the first quilt, but you are building on what you learned while making it. In other words, you have a head start on the learning process. The design, theme, or color choices may unite your series. As you begin your second piece you're starting in the middle, rather than at the beginning of a new design concept. There's nothing wrong with repeating ideas, especially if they are good ones.

While I am working on a quilt, my mind is bombarded with a variety of ideas and questions: What if I changed this, what if I added that, how would it look in other colors? As I work on one quilt, ideas for the next quilt are percolating away. When I work in a series I explore these kindred ideas. I may begin with units akin to the original, but they will never be the same. Differences arise in the structure of the units, the color scheme, or the block placement. Whatever the changes, the new quilt will be decidedly different from the one before. This metamorphosis takes place when you continue to experiment with design and explore all the possibilities.

Worlds Apart III
Sandi Cummings
54" x 54", private collection.
Photo by Don Tuttle

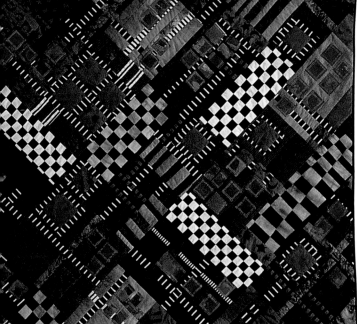

Night Shades
Sandi Cummings
48" x 42", quilted by Sandy Klop,
corporate collection.
Photo by Joseph Untalan

As you work on pieces in a series you clarify your ideas and style. What you really like and don't like becomes clearer. As a result, your work will become stronger. We've all looked at a finished quilt and wished we had done something different. It's all a part of the process of learning to be creative. Working in a series is your chance to improve and refine your ideas.

Desert Shades, Sandi Cummings, 42" x 48", quilted by Sandy Klop, corporate collection. Photo by Joseph Untalan

Detail of *Night Shades*

Tip: I like to use striped fabric on a piece of fabric that is one of the colors in the stripe. When it is inserted it makes the other stripes look like they are floating. (See Night Shades detail.)

Collaborative Quilting

Quilting can be a solitary activity. Collaboration is a way to add creative spark and depth to your work. "Two heads are better than one" often rings true. There are various ways to work with another quilter on a project: you might make sections and trade them, work on two quilts simultaneously, or make one quilt between you.

It's important to collaborate with someone you are compatible with. You need to have confidence in your partner's sense of color and design and generally respect her work. Try to work with someone who is open to give and take, and whose work ethic is similar to your own. It's important that both of you follow through with your share of the work and be committed to completing the project.

The first time I collaborated with my friend Sandy Klop we decided to work together in the same studio. The goal was to make two

Lilies, Sandi Cummings and Anne Hunter Hamilton, 43" x 40". This quilt was made in collaboration with Anne Hunter Hamilton, a painter. Anne gave me one of her paintings to cut up and combine with fabrics.

quilts so we would each have one to keep when we were finished. After about two hours it was pretty clear that the quilt to the left on the design wall was her project and the one on the right was mine. We never really worked on both together. She worked on hers and I worked on mine. We talked and occasionally gave suggestions to each other on color and fabric placement, but basically our work remained separate.

Ode to a Lady, Sandi Cummings, 46" x 43", corporate collection. This was our first non-collaborative collaboration. Who else but quilters could use floral lips and eyebrows?
Photo by Joseph Untalan

Sandy and I analyzed the process and decided in subsequent quilts to work together and produce one quilt. That method has been much more successful for us. We discuss ideas for subject matter ahead of time and both come with suggestions. After we have agreed on our subject, often inspired by a photo, we work together on fabric selection and the design approach.

We agree that working together is a productive and energizing experience. We share the excitement of success as the piece evolves, as well as the frustration of setbacks when we're not happy with what we've accomplished. Collaborating pushes us to try things we might not otherwise try and demands that we be open to someone else's ideas and solutions. We also have to be willing to compromise since we both have strong ideas about what we like and dislike. The decision usually goes to the person who feels the strongest about an issue at the time. It isn't necessarily that we resist working with the other person's approach; just that we have

Woman in Repose, Sandi Cummings and Sandy Klop, 53" x 76". The background is made up of double-cut large rectangles. Photo by Don Tuttle

developed our own way of working and resist what does not come naturally. Sandy and I make quilts together that we would never make on our own. We particularly enjoy the process of fabric selection since Sandy and I each purchase very different fabrics.

Sisters, Sandi Cummings and Sandy Klop, 68" x 56". These women were very fun to dress. Photo by Don Tuttle

Our working styles are somewhat different. Sandy tends to work much faster and unrestrained, while I am slower and more deliberate. She may want to move on and resolve a problem later, while I might choose to rework an area at the time. When working together we adjust to a middle ground that combines the best of both approaches.

Occasionally when I am trying to solve a design problem of my own, I think of Sandy Klop. Since no two people work and think exactly alike, it is a good exercise to question what someone else would do to solve a design problem. Collaboration can expand your thinking and get you working outside of your box.

Quilting has become a rather solitary activity. We often sit at home and work on our projects in isolation. Collaborating gives you shared enthusiasm, a shared vision, and a new voice.

New York City Garden, Sandi Cummings and Sandy Klop, 79" x 67".
Sandy and I worked from a photo I took while visiting New York City.

it *talk* over

It's fun to work on a quilt and watch it develop, but sometimes you want to spark your creativity by getting together with other quilters for ideas and inspiration. Aside from providing needed companionship, fellow quilters can help you refine and improve your work through critiquing.

Starting a Group

Finding or starting a group can be a rewarding experience. I belong to one that has provided invaluable help over the years, largely because members have set guidelines for our critiques and dialogues. It's not easy to ask for critical comments about your work, no matter how helpful they may turn out to be. Here are some guidelines for eliciting useful suggestions and avoiding bruised egos and hurt feelings.

Setting Goals

Discuss why you are forming or joining the group. Talk about the expectations of members and what they hope to get from and give to the group.

In most groups members will have different levels of experience in quilting and in presenting their work to others. Consider the individual differences as you critique. In a small, on-going group, try to be sensitive to the personalities of the members. Some are more receptive to feedback than others. Believe that everyone is capable of making good quilts. We all have ability and talent, and are simply at different levels in our artistic development. Group members should recognize

this and make it a safe place to show any works in progress and seek informed reactions to them. All dialogue should be based on mutual respect and supportive, helpful input.

Talk about what you see going on in various parts of the quilt. When critiquing you can go back to some of the issues you have addressed in your own work, such as value, scale, and balance. What kind of an emotional response does the work elicit?

Offer positive and affirming comments about the strong attributes of a quilt. Point out areas you particularly like. These comments are very important because they help build the artist's confidence and let her know what areas to focus on and emphasize or perhaps to explore further.

Try to frame your comments about weaker areas in a way that promotes creative thinking and discussion. Feedback that comes across as negative is not helpful because it may stifle discussion. It isn't that you are avoiding the issue or misleading the artist, but a comment such as "I don't like that part" effectively cuts off dialogue. You are placing your power of observation over hers. Perhaps that part of the quilt is her favorite. A more helpful comment might be, "I really like the color and strength you have on the left side of the quilt, and I feel the upper right-hand area is not as strong." This approach encourages discussion and leaves the quilter in charge of considering alternatives. After all, she will ultimately be the one to decide what to change, and whether to accept or reject suggestions.

I remember a time when I felt closed down by a few comments. I was selecting fabric for a class and the instructor criticized what I had chosen for an accent. Although I thought it was a good choice, she did not like it and felt that it would never work. Since she was the teacher and I was the student, I felt it was no longer okay for me to use that fabric. If she had suggested a change in value, color, or whatever, I would have explored the options. I might have considered changing something else so the original fabric could work, but that criticism made me feel the teacher had already decided for me. She had taken away my permission to use that particular fabric. I believe the quiltmaker should always be the one to make the final decisions about her work.

When pieces are being shown to the group, notice the artist's presentation: Is she happy with the piece, or wondering if more work is needed? Likewise, realize that not every quilt we make is a great work of art. Some will be better than others. Even if you don't complete a piece, or it doesn't work out as successfully as you planned, you have learned something valuable. These experiences are necessary to grow and change directions with our art.

Agree to share something each time you meet. If you haven't had a chance to work on a quilt, bring a new book, drawing, painting, or something else that interests or inspires you.

Take this opportunity to discuss technical issues, new products, and upcoming shows and lectures, for art in general as well as quilt art. In my group we have brought in guest teachers and held fabric dyeing retreats.

Shows or Exhibits

Consider organizing a show. There are many opportunities for groups to exhibit these days. Exhibits are a vehicle for celebrating the diversity and accomplishments of the group, as well as a personal opportunity for exposure of your own work. Sometimes it is easier to represent and promote the efforts of a group rather than your own work. In order to present a group proposal to a gallery or corporation, you should have a small portfolio or binder that includes the artists' resumes or artists' statements and photographs representative of each member's work. A business card for the group also inspires legitimacy.

Suggestions for You

When you show a quilt to your group, let them know how far along it is. Comments will differ depending on whether you are halfway through it and looking for lots of input, or nearly done. Remember that if you show a work in progress you may receive premature criticism. To elicit helpful comments you may want to ask questions like "I'm having trouble with this section, do you have any ideas?" or "Do you notice anything that stands out and needs fixing?"

Suggested solutions to technical problems can be especially helpful. There are so many new products and methods available it is almost impossible to keep up with new developments. You'll be surprised how much time you can save with shortcuts you learn from others.

Ask the group to brainstorm with you on solving design problems. I find it really opens up my thinking process to toss around ideas, even if they may seem far-fetched. You may often end up not using any of those exact ideas, but they may lead you to your own solution.

In addition to the helpful feedback I have received from my group, it has been an education for me just to see the growth and development in the work of the individual members during the years we have been meeting.

Talk About Your Quilts

Learn to talk about your quilts. Early in my quilting career someone asked me what I was trying to express with my quilts. I was totally unprepared to answer that question. As I thought about it, I realized that I wanted my quilts to have depth, space, and a feeling of strength. That question made me think about how to articulate what I was trying to do with my quilts. Some people find it helpful to write an artist's statement about their work. Whether you actually write it down or verbalize it, describing your intent makes you think critically about your work and helps provide a clear focus.

Set personal goals for what you want to accomplish by the next meeting. This is something that my contemporary quilt group did when we first started meeting. We no longer do this, probably because we are all committed quilters and try hard to bring new work to each meeting. However, committing to a goal can be an effective way to keep on track and move toward completion of a project.

Moving away from traditional quilt patterns and into designing your own quilts can be both freeing and unsteadying. We all like to know we are on the right track and to hear positive statements and encouraging words from fellow quilters. Positive feedback is one of the many things that encourages and revitalizes us as we move forward in our creative growth.

A Moment in Time, Sandi Cummings, 84" x 60", corporate collection. The floating triangles work as connectors from one panel to another and add a spark of color. Photo by Don Tuttle

Resources

Pro Chemical & Dye Inc.
P. O. Box 14
Somerset, MA 02726
(508) 676-3838
1-800-2-BUY-DYE - Orders only

www.prochemical.com

Procion MX dyes and Synthrapol
(used after dyeing
fabric, to wash out excess loose
dye particles)

Dharma Trading Co.
P.O. Box 150916
San Rafael, CA 94917
Telephone (415) 456-7657
(800) 542-5227

www.dharmatrading.com

Procion MX dyes, fabric ready
for dyeing, and Synthrapol

Testfabrics, Inc.
415 Delaware Ave., P. O. Box 26
West Pittston, PA 18643
(570) 603-0432
Fax (570) 603-0433

Fabric ready for dyeing. I use
419 bleached, mercerized
combed cotton broadcloth.

Ann Johnston, Color by Accident,
self-published.

About the Authors

Sandi Cummings balances her time between local teaching, a national lecture/workshop schedule, and, most importantly, her art quilt creations. Sandi's work has been juried into many prestigious art quilt shows, including Visions, Women of Taste, and Quilt National. She has numerous pieces in both personal and corporate collections. Sandi resides in Moraga, California.

Sandi is drawn to quilting by the opportunity to blend the warm and tactile properties of fabric with the richness of color and patterning. She believes that fabric art is a woman's heritage, and enjoys being part of that group of artists who have chosen to express themselves with original designs in cloth and thread. For her, quilts and other fabric art represent the quiet strength of women and the caring side of humanity. They are symbolic of how dedicated women attempt to bring beauty to the home and family and to our everyday lives. In keeping with that spirit, she wants her work to be affirmative, and to reflect vitality and strength. Visit Sandi at sandicummings.com.

Karen Flamme has combined an avocation as a fiber artist with a lengthy career as a writer and producer of award-winning corporate communications. Her embellished garments and textile creations were sold under the Thread Bear label. Karen turned to quilting a decade ago, and her quilts are exhibited and in private collections. Her work recently appeared in Art Quilts: Encrustations, A Cut Above, and the Houston International Quilt Festival. Karen resides in Oakland and Pebble Beach, California.

The continual exploration of color, texture, and design—both in art and language—are fascinating to Karen. She sees self-expression as an essential part of an individual's growth and development, whether through words, art, music, or movement. She believes that quilts and handwork passed down through the generations are the foundation of this art form upon which quilters can now experiment to find their own voices.

Index

For more information, ask for a free catalog:
C&T Publishing, Inc.
P.O. Box 1456
Lafayette, CA 94549
(800) 284-1114
Email: ctinfo@ctpub.com
Website: www.ctpub.com

For quilting supplies:
Cotton Patch Mail Order
3405 Hall Lane, Dept. CTB
Lafayette, CA 94549
(800) 835-4418
(925) 283-7883
Email: quiltusa@yahoo.com
Website: www.quiltusa.com

Note: Fabrics used in the quilts shown may
not be currently available because fabric
manufacturers keep most fabrics in print for
only a short time.